CU00946956

# GAY & TIRED

Quips & Pieces

On Modern Gay Love

By Topher Gen

Copyright 2018

Book cover design

by **Daniel Tyminski**

Queer artist and illustrator

from Scotland living in London.

www.dtyminski.co.uk

@dtyminskidraws

# Contents

# *Section I*

# Dating &

# Disappointment

# Modern Gay Love.

Dating in your twenties will have you alternating between rage, jealousy, bewilderment and distress. Sometimes it's utterly authentic doom incarnate. It makes you feel as though you were born without laugh muscles and raised in a civilization that never invented the smile. Nobody does face-to-face disappointment quite like gay romance.

There are days when I feel I am one failed romance away from being sent to the dating equivalent of the Shadow Realm; there are times when I am both needy and unavailable and there's been hours when I wasn't sure if I was falling in love with a guy, or just needed to masturbate. I'm either aggressively playing house because I'm scared of what an uncertain time it is, or I'm avoiding commitment altogether. Gay dating is a paragon of uncertainty.

One thing I know unequivocally is that my desperation to meet someone, to fall in love, can blind me from certain realities – like it has for so many others. We want a partner so badly, but don't think for a second that maybe the guy we're 'seeing' isn't currently equipped to handle anything romantic. It's this unquenchable thirst for a boyfriend that often causes us to rush into the wrong dates/relationships. Then, when they implode, we're left with the ignominy of having to explain to our friends why this one didn't work out – honestly, we don't know.  The trouble with desperation is it often stops us seeing our own worth – which is a bit of an issue.

I do think that gay guys in their twenties accept a lesser

treatment than they would at any other point in their lives. How many of us put up with subpar behaviour from people we've dated? How many times have we continued to give someone a second, third, sometimes a fourth chance after they've treated us like dirt? How many times have you been out with a guy that's treated you like a taxi driver and had entire conversations in front of you like you're invisible?

So, why do we put up with it? Why don't we just sit down and patiently wait on the right guy coming along? Undoubtedly age is one reason for this. Age and time. Time is ticking out, quickly find a husband, find a husband! Some days I wake up and think this aging process is kicking my ass harder than Ebola. Growing old feels 2,000 times worse for gay men; it's an entirely alternate dimension of shit than it is for straight people. You're a twink, then you blink and suddenly you've been blasted to the far corners of a galaxy full of regret, saggy bellies, reddish skin & constant streams of rejection.

We live in a community that praises the youthful and banishes the old to the decrepit corners of seedy bars where they sit gathering dust and consolidating all their regrets into one manageable block of misery. Like it or not appearance is major player in the dating game; if you've got the looks and youthful charm, then the odds are in your favour. It'll be easier to snare a husband or a boyfriend or whatever it is you're after. A direct reaction to having this mindset is what causes a growing pressure to be put on gay guys to find a partner whilst we're still young. This in turn leads to us going on aforementioned wrong dates; it sees us investing energy in the wrong people, which wastes more time, which causes us to panic more, and thus the cycle repeats. I don't get it. It's as though the moment we hit 34 we automatically get removed from the meat market and are put out to pasture like one of those cows that's too old to produce milk anymore.

This nasty age prejudice that's swimming about causes mass panic. It makes us worry that we won't find someone in time - in time for what though? The world isn't going to end any time soon, so what's the rush? Well, our rapidly dwindling looks for starters.

As the infamous Mrs Wormwood once said to her weird daughter's teacher, '*You chose books – I chose looks!*' They say beauty is in the eye of the beholder, which is a shame because this week the Nation Guild of Beholders sent me a direct message on Twitter telling me I've got a face like a rucksack full of dented bells. And before one of you rolls their eyes into the next street, that 'personality is what matters' malarkey doesn't fly with me – it's just a lie they tell us ugly people to stop us from rioting. Personality of course does come into play, but sadly it isn't what most guys go for. I've met guys with hearts of gold, but they didn't whip me into a sexual frenzy – and a lot of us need that in a relationship.

Another reason we put up with some seriously stinking BS is sometimes we convince ourselves that the guy we're dating is someone, rather something, that he's not. It's a tough pill to swallow, but the idea of someone is often more appealing than the reality.

The idolisation of men based on the traits you want them to have, as opposed to their actual traits (which at first you're too blind to see) is one that leads to a lot of issues. Especially when it comes to dating. If we'd only take a step back we'd notice that we've fallen for someone that doesn't exist. Sure, he's pleasant enough, but so are chicken pakora, so why are we letting him away with treating us this bad?

How many of us date guys and excuse their shitty behaviour? *He wouldn't cheat, he didn't mean to snap, he's too busy to reply…*I've been there, so I am not judging. I was shown multiple receipts and still reused to believe my ex was cheating on me. The thing a lot of guys don't realise is enduring this sort of treatment is so detrimental to their health – both mentally and physically. If someone treats you in a terrible way for long enough you eventually start to believe you deserve it. That parts of you aren't good enough to be loved; that aspects of yourself are less endearing than others. When that happens you stop being a whole person, you break into tiny bits. That's when you start hating parts of yourself. But you're not made up of compartments, you're a full person! And every bit of you deserves to be loved.

Here are typical examples of modern love; routine pitstops on the search for your soul mate: Someone not texting back, growing anxious whilst waiting on a reply; augmenting aspects of yourself just so they mimic a guy's preferences. Your style, music tastes and favourite movies, suddenly they better match his. We get carried away with possibility; we picture our future based on what other people have. We want to skip to the good part, the commitment, but we don't want to put the work in. We move too fast at the start of a relationship and after a few weeks it implodes - when really love is something you need to build slowly, because pop-up love never lasts. It's good at the time, but it can't weather a storm.

At the end of the day, there will always be guys that have a PHD in mixed signals; they'll say what you want to hear to get what they want – which I'm assuming is mostly sex. I just wish guys could work out the difference between having feelings and wanting to get off. There are certain situations that no matter how hard you try, you can't navigate elegantly or easily, but there's a certain grace to having your heart broken – and from each bad date and failed romance, we can learn something.

# The Honesty Trick.

When it comes to dating guys, it's all about honesty. A lack of honesty in the early stages of a relationship is what stops it from growing and may causes us to land in sticky situations (and not the favourable kind.). Why? Because *'Honesty is the best policy.'*

That's one gem of wisdom my gran imparted, along with *'Watch Absolutely Fabulous when you're sad'* and *'It's shoes or go barefoot, never wear espadrilles.'* Then again, this was also the woman who was adamant that if I applied myself daily then I would become successful famous – and she wasn't playing. My grandma was like Tiger Wood's daddy, always pressuring.

The first slice of wisdom is a bit of a blanket statement but, depending on the situation, it can make sense. The other two? Well, they're rules I follow with an almost religious-like devotion (we'll ignore the other bit.)

Honesty is a tricky thing to get right, so think of it as a balancing procedure. Applied correctly, the right amount can resolve situations with minimum upset and little guilt; but if you're brash or too honest, or honest at the wrong times, then you may wind up getting booed to death or bitch slapped.

When it comes to dating, feelings, and all matters love, I always prefer honesty. If someone's not into you, that's fine. They're clearly a faulty, emotionless robot, but it's totally fine. For most of us though, particularly gay men, I think honesty is a concept we struggle to grasp. We shy away from honesty as it's often synonymous with responsibility – and we all like to avoid that.

Couple of tips: If you *don't* know what you want, refrain from booting someone's heart in the balls and don't sleep with them. Keep it in your pants. Make sure *you're* sure. Also, watch out for those guys that think with their penis, it doesn't point in the direction of sense. You know the type, the ones that leave a cum trail wherever they go, kind of like a slutty slug.

# Menthol Cigarettes.

I want a boyfriend. Any boyfriend. And this boy, the one with a cute-but-handsome little face attached to a toned body, fits my idea nicely. Initially I only liked his Instagram; then I started to appreciate his quirky web presence and his endearingly blunt replies. Then, before I knew it, it soon became him I liked.

Eventually we stitched together a plan for what was to be our first 'official' date: I was to make us dinner on the Friday and I was going to be meticulous to the last detail. I would present myself in a way that came across grateful, but also casual; I'd be keen and into it but also balanced and laid back. I needed this to be perfect.

Friday came, but when I messaged him to confirm a time I was met with his trademark silence. I paced about, waiting on his reply, while picturing our hypothetical relationship together – and the thoughts played out in my head like a cinematic daydream. Our first kiss, the first night he'd stay over, the moment we'd move beyond this and into something tangible, real. I was letting myself run away with what was little more than possibilities – as many of us do.

A few minutes dragged by and the status of my message changed to 'read.' My heart skipped. I wasn't head-over-heels for this guy, but every time we spoke it felt as though I was about to go on the best vacation of my life. I braced myself and watched as those little iPhone dots popped up; the ones that tantalizingly tell you someone is typing their response. The mobile phone equivalent of a slow climb to the top of a rollercoaster. A moment later those hopeful dots vanished.

Maybe he's just crafting a response and wasn't happy with it? Perhaps he wants his reply to be perfect? Or doesn't want to come across over eager? I tried to soothe myself with excuses; I settled on he's probably busy – but being too busy to reply is as redundant an excuse as my dog ate my homework. Slowly my confidence in us started dwindling and shifting into doubt. Then reality hit: he's going to cancel.

We were two weeks deep into the 'getting to know each other' stage when I noticed he had an attitude that said he was equal parts interested and unavailable. It was then that it dawned on me that I've been here before. Swooning after someone that only leaves me with an empty fluish feeling; seeking satisfaction by wanting what I can't have, much like I couldn't have him. I should have called it off there and then, but I didn't. I wish my future self could have sent some sort of smoke signal telling me to run from what was blatantly going to be another failed romance.

An hour later, he cancelled. He didn't offer an explanation, just a basic, quickly-crafted reply. I could feel in that one sentence an essential indifference towards me that was neither merited or explained.  Later that afternoon I saw he was in my city and this information sat with me like a bad meal.

I walked around the rest of the day like I'd seen a ghost - another haunting visit from rejection. This sensation crushed down on my shoulders, and after that trying to keep my mood positive felt a lot like swimming with rocks strapped to my ankles.

The thing is, we only met in person a few times and there wasn't any natural spark. Each time we met my conversational skills went from razor sharp to dull and blunt in 0.4 seconds – and talking to someone you like should never feel forced.

After each encounter I convinced myself he was special, because I wanted him to be special. I was so taken by *everything* about him. His fresh style, his tanned complexion; by the way he'd stuff a pack of menthols into the front pocket of his acid-wash denim jacket, and how that complimented his nonchalant demeanour perfectly.

I was so hypnotized by his beauty that I couldn't look at him directly. I was scared he'd realise that he could do better; I was worried he'd be turned off by the fact I can't edit my face in real life, so I spent more time looking at the ground than into his eyes. I just panicked and started worrying he'd look at me as though I was a ridiculously hairy beast with the face of a Picasso painting. I'd fallen for an idea, an image, not a real person.

There are brief periods where I convince myself that something will work before I even know the person; and when it crumbles, when it fails, the disappointment is amplified. I did this with the guy I'm writing about. I created scenarios where we'd be compatible; I imagined ways in which we'd work. But when I think about the truth of the matter I shudder at the thought: None of it was real. I romanticized everything.

In the draft of this essay I mentioned this guy by using a single letter, as though addressing him in that way would be romantic, but it's not. It was just a further attempt to make something that meant nothing mean something.

Investing time and energy in the wrong people is a frequent mistake of mine, and it's one that fills me with so much frustration I want to punch a hole in the wall. Instead of asking 'why don't you love me?' I should be asking: 'are you worthy of my love?'

## First.

On September 13th, 2011, I got an alert from Facebook pinged to my mobile. At the time I didn't own a fancy iPhone, so all I received was a frantic beeping sound and a text that told me I had a mail. It was from my 'ex-boyfriend'. I use that term loosely because even though we technically weren't ever a couple, I had invested a lot, both emotionally and psychically, into the relationship. The subject was headed 'PLEASE READ THIS.' which is the universal code for '*You probably don't want to read this*'. With great curiosity and a little nausea, I clicked on the message. He'd broke up with me. Via Facebook.

I can only compare this feeling to opening a biscuit jar but instead of being greeted by cookies you get cock-slapped.

One of the saddest feelings in life is when you're dancing in a really joyful way, totally absorbed in the music, then you hit your head. Another is when you start feeling sexy then trip. The worst is having someone you love dismiss years of effort as casually as a used tea bag.

I was dumfounded, confused. I was so angry that I was shaking. A sickly knot-in-my-stomach tightened at the thought that I wouldn't be able to see or touch him again. I wanted to write 'ARE YOU FUCKING SERIOUS?' I wanted to yell at him. 'WE HAD SEX TWO NIGHTS AGO AND I PAID FOR ALL YOUR DRINKS!' But I couldn't. I couldn't write anything. Because he had blocked me.

I called my friend Chole who was in college at the time. With a levelheadedness that was foreign for her she asked me to explain, in detail, what happened. This was ironic because every one of my friends saw this coming – this was just the inevitable outcome to a very blatant situation for them.

A few months later my friend had left her Facebook account logged on, so with zero hesitation I started to creep on my ex's page. Slowly I started catching up on the last four months of his life, refreshing his page as thoughtlessly as some twirl their hair. Then I saw he'd posted that he'd moved away. I was livid. He moved away? And he didn't even fucking tell me? After me moaning for weeks that I wished he'd move away so I didn't have to worry about bumping into him and he's now gone and done it? For a while I carried about so much self-pity that it gave me a limp. And so began the first ever real heartache I ever had.

Years later and that muscle in my chest, which I thought would have withered and died by now, is still taking knocks and fractures but beating steadily on.

After a bad breakup it's amazingly interesting how we

often can't see the ways in which we are being strong – you aren't aware that what you're doing is tough and brave at the time, but you're doing it. You're surviving one of the toughest rides and most potent pains you'll ever face. And just because you don't know it's bravery, it doesn't mean it isn't. If you knew you were being brave, then you'd probably be scared.

## Clingy.

I am often called clingy. By strangers, by guys, by friends I relentlessly moan at. I guess it's because I have two settings when it comes to dating. The first sees me carry a general sense of indifference about the relationship until it morphs into a crippling boredom, by which point I feel too guilty to end things. The second setting sees me planning our honeymoon before the guy's finished his coffee on our first date. There is no middle; I either have bucket loads of chill or absolutely zero.

When it's the first I'm easy going. I breeze through the entire relationship regardless of what that lifespan may be. I don't freak when they don't text back right away; I'm casual, laid back, and I'm nonchalant about sex and stuff. I become the person I hate in relationships. Then there's setting number two, which sees my aggressive clinginess inevitability asphyxiate the relationship. Then I transform into a forlorn creature who gnaws away at slices of pizza without guilt or remorse after tanning a litre of gin with a dash of despair as mixer. Then, when I'm drunk enough, I leap back on Tinder because it's simple and not serious; it's the ultimate gamification of romance. It's 'Pokémon Go' for the heart.

## Gays in Common.

Social Media and Twitter make it too easy to navel-gaze in way we never have before. Every time I see another guy get into a relationship, or a couple digitally documenting a milestone, I'm a boiling pot of envy.

I think back to all the dates and accumulated months of 'seeing' guys that have amounted to little more than disappointment and think 'What if?' What if we had worked and it was us clogging up other peoples' timeline with our bilious happiness? Then, mid-stalk, you see someone you once dated shamelessly flirting with someone else you got head from. Even more unsettling, they've posted a selfie together! So, you sit and wait, praying the full time this flirting implodes because that way the issue was them and not you.

Dating in the gay world is inherently difficult. I'd go as far as to say that it's harder than it is for heterosexual couples. Most guys I meet and date spring into my life via the gay scene, which is a problem. If you live in a smallish city like I do (Glasgow) then chances are you're going to meet someone with whom you have 'gays in common'.

GIC (gays in common) is a little game I like to play. The first part involves you both swiping through Facebook to see what homosexual friends you have in common. For the second part, you get to sit and decipher which ones he's slept with, only going by his facial expressions and the amount/lack of eye contact he makes.

The game is risky because there's a high probability that you've shared one, if not more, sexual partners. Or it'll turn out you've been with someone who's been with someone that they've been with. It's all horribly incestuous and seedy. The whole thing instils a sense of cheapness over the whole relationship before you've even made it to the second date. I'm always left thinking, I don't share my food so why would I share my sexual partner?

## Just a Number.

I go on dates with younger guys because it's cheaper as they only want a Happy Meal when I take them to McDonald's – totally kidding. I've dated younger guys but often it's left me disheartened as they are still at the stage I was at a few years ago: where you just want to have fun. They also make me jealous because I can't wear crop-tops anymore. They also hammer in a sense of dread when I realise I'm getting older. It also makes me panic a little bit that suddenly I'm not 'cool' anymore. As if in the last twenty seconds I've transformed into this prehistoric dad-like creature that stomps around like a T-rex, muttering things that are no longer said or relevant.

I go on dates with older guys and find it hard to navigate

18

the conversation or translate the generational gap. The last two proper dates I went on were with guys younger than me, and it quickly morphed into a hook-up after a few drinks. The one prior to that was with someone fourteen-years older. Now, I thought it went well, until the next morning when I awoke to a text saying he found my 'constant' social media presence offensive and it wasn't for him. I hate the idea of offending people, so I quickly unlinked my Twitter from my Facebook…then tweeted about the incident. I guess I like to have my cake and Tweet it too.

Then I try to date someone the same age as me, only to find myself shrinking into my seat as they list all their accomplishments then drop the dreaded 'I've got a mortgage' bomb while I simultaneously try to hide the fact I still have Pokémon Go on my phone.

## No.

The number of guys I've spoken to that have recanted scenarios befitting the label of sexual assault is disgusting. Last year I woke up to a guy having sex with me. No sex isn't the right word, because that sounds as though I made an educational choice, when really it didn't feel like a choice at all. I'd passed out (drunk) and woke up disorientated only to quickly sober up when I realised that this guy was, for lack of a better term, inside me. I said stop, he kept going. I said stop again, he covered my mouth – as if this was some sort of fetish for him, when really it was one thing and one thing only: Rape.

His excuse was, '*I've not got many gay friends, this is a learning curve for me.*' Two questions: **1**) Would your female friends wake up to you being balls deep in their vagina? I     didn't think so. **2**) Do you want me to cut off your hands and fashion them into whimsical candle holders? No? Well, keep them to yourself in the future.

This ties back to what I was saying earlier about needing to be in a relationship. We put ourselves in a dangerous situation and as such can get burned – and sadly I know a lot of gay men that have suffered similar, if not worse, situations to mine. This is in fact alarmingly common, and yet as men the term 'rape' seems humiliating.

No means no. It doesn't mean try again in five-to-fifteen minutes; it doesn't mean reapply for a permit in six-to-ten working days and most certain does not mean do it anyway!

We wouldn't let friends treat us this way, so why do we let guys do it? Just because they're offering the possibility of attention or even love? It's like, someone won't message us back or will chose when it suits him to flirt or sleep with us and we just let it happen.

We need to stop enduring behaviour we'd tell our friends wasn't acceptable. We need to love ourselves and in order for that to happen we need to change what we see in the mirror. A boyfriend would be great; a partner is the goal – but we are more important than those two things.

# End Game.

So, what are our actions are motored by? Why do we go on dates? I hate dating, but I'm awful at it so I go because I need the practice. Is it a quest to find a boyfriend or a husband? Something to do? Someone to do?

Every time I see a child and its parents I'm left wondering if I'm going to have a family of my own in the future. Will I meet the right guy and have a fancy house or finally land in a place of financial security? Maybe even get a dog or twelve! But if all my decisions are influenced by the promise of gaining one, if not all, of the above, then what am I doing wrong?

That *'You'll meet the right guy when you least expect it'* nonsense really annoys me – it's about as helpful as pubic lice. Just tell me where I am going wrong! Am I looking in the wrong places? Is there a glittery rock somewhere that all the good gays are hiding under?

How many times have you met a great guy, but they aren't psychically your type? People call that shallow, but you need to be sexuality attracted to the person. Then the flip side of this is you meet a guy that just wants sex and he turns out to be such a slut that you need an antibiotic for just sitting in his car. Dating only seems to result in the same way: me lying alone in my bed, pregnant with crisps. Probably wanking. Maybe sleeping or watching Buffy episodes.

# *Section II*

# Body & Sex

# Like a Virgin.

Being ready to lose your virginity was a lot like when you were a child and got invited to a sleepover. Every week people would have them, they were all the rage. And every week I'd be like *'No, I don't want to sleepover. I want my mum, my own bed, my own sheets.'* I'd be mocked every time I declined, but whatever; I wasn't ready. Staying over was a big commitment.

Then one day someone asked again, but this time I was like *'yes!'* and suddenly I was filled with an urge to be there. That's what it felt like for me. I was terrified for so long and, even though all my peers were doing it, I kept shying away. Then one night – at a sleepover – it happened because I felt ready. After that I was the fucking sleepover king.

People tend to think the first time you have sex with another guy will be painful; as though someone's trying to drive a train through your asshole. But the emotional intensity of my first time trumped that pain – and all I kept thinking was *'fuck, this is happening. Fuck, fuck, fuck!'* Here's a brief encounter of that night.

My first time wasn't romantic. It happened on a worn-out sofa and, like many of us, it was with a straight guy. I went over to stay at this boy's house and things proceeded as normal. Computer games, food, the most mundane and basic of teen chat. We managed to steal some vodka and it felt like a warm hug of confidence sliding down my throat.

After the allure of the Xbox subsided, and the alcohol kicked in, we started playing truth or dare. Each round we'd push each other to take swigs of alcohol, dance stupidly or prank call someone. Then the truth's subsided and the dares evolved. Before I knew it, we were having sex.

The whole encounter was as divorced of romance as you can get. He kissed me like it was a chore and removed my underwear with indifference. Looking back, I'm still kind of pissed about how blasé he was.

I clung to him, figuring he would tell me if this was what sex was meant to feel like. By his own admission, he had done this before with another guy. He pushed my head into the pillow and arched my back and after a few stutters and starts, we got a flow. I don't know what I was expecting it to feel like, but it was not this. It was not elegant (imagine someone was trying to thread the eye of a needle with a cucumber.)

As it continued he started to make a few weird grunting noises, like a distressed farm animal or Serena Williams when she's serving; I honestly was waiting for him to yell 'Hulk smash!' at one point. Then, a moment later, it was over, and it was the most grotesque sound I have ever heard – imagine someone throwing a squid against a glass wall.

After a couple weeks he stopped wanting to spend time with me. After a couple months he joined my lynch mob and looked at me with the same disdain as the other straight boys. Eventually he got violent and gave me a black eye – also my first.

After being dicked for the first time and being dismally left at the side of the road (metaphorically, I waddled home the next day) I decided that I would only ever lean towards guys I thought could be into me too. It's not till later in life that I realised that some guys are just after sex – and sadly that doesn't seem to change with age.

I figure for a lot of gay guys the first time you have sex is a pivotal moment, because it's in that moment – that often painful, embarrassing, moment – you realise that this is what other guys are after. For many of us we carry this forward, and unwittingly use sex as a way of keeping someone interested. Sex can be fun, but it can also be a weapon; worse still, it can do some serious emotional damage. My advice would be: It doesn't matter how many times you've done it in the past, when it comes to someone new make sure you're ready before sleeping with him. More importantly: respect yourself enough by making sure he's deserving of your body.

## Everybody Loves Cake.

The first time I ever heard the term 'eating disorder' I was around the age of 11. I'd dived into one of my mother's magazines and in the middle of it was an article accompanied by upsetting images of emaciated girls with folded hands and hollow-looking eyes.

I didn't know what anorexia or bulimia was at that point; all I knew was those girls looked hungry and sad and bony. After chewing on the information for a while I took away two things from the article: 1) Eating disorders only affect girls and 2) I didn't want to catch anorexia. Because it was a disease, right?

Nobody bothered to explain to me at the time that you

didn't just become bulimic or anorexic overnight; and thus, I added getting an eating disorder to my ever-growing shelf of childish-fears, sitting it neatly between a smallpox outbreak and having to do 'show and tell' in front of my primary school class.    I    didn't know it at the time, but that article had planted a seed that would over the years bloat into a glutinous paranoia about my own weight.

The first time I weighed myself I wasn't yet a teenager. Some pre-pubescent urge to check what I weighed crept in one day and after that I began to weigh myself often. My mum kept this battery-operated relic from the 80s underneath her bed. Once a week I'd go to her room, kick my shoes off and grow impatient at the ten-second lag it took for the numbers to appear. That was the first step down the very slippery slope that lead directly to my eating disorder.

Recently, I watched a documentary on BBC 3 called Queer Britain and it raised the issue of body dysmorphia amongst men, and gay men in particular. It really clawed away at me and dug up a lot of old feelings. It hammered home that despite eating disorders becoming increasingly common amongst gay men, we parade around the idea of a 'perfect' body despite how toxic a notion it is.

I've wobbled between both sides of the judgmental seesaw at various points. I've been mocked for being too thin and was made to feel like less of a man for because my frame looked feminine. When I was at my biggest, I had nasty comments made about my body; remarks that clung to the layer of stubborn belly fat I was carrying around and really weighed me down.

The first set of comments made me feel less masculine and as though being a feminine guy was a bad thing. The second tipped the scales and imbued me with a potent sense of self-loathing that made feel as though I had the sexual allure of a warthog.

I have ridden the yo-yo diet for years. On one end I was ramming my fingers down my throat in order to lose the weight faster; and the other saw the lower half of my body stretched out under running water whilst the upper half was slung over the side of the bath eating a loaf of bread.

I've had months that were an orgy of takeaways and multipacks of crisps; eating that fifth slice of pizza that was both unwanted and unneeded, using grief management as my excuse. There was the period where, despite being 10lbs underweight, I still saw Jabba the Hut belly-dancing back at me any time I looked in a mirror. Bulimia, anorexia – any eating disorder – are lonely diseases. They are lonelier still for the guys that suffer from them.

The pressure and prejudice we have about body image in the gay community is toxic. The irony of having shady comments thrown at you by a community that is formed on a solid foundation of inclusion and acceptance has not been lost on me.

We femme shame all the time whilst simultaneously not replying to the bigger guy that messaged us on Grindr. It's rock-hard abs and rippling pectorals or nothing – both on our partner, and on ourselves. This 'perfect' image gay men pursue is so damaging yet we don't see it. I used to think that if I ate some broccoli and did some crunches then my abs would turn up with an army of potential suitors behind them, but you can't just pull the 'perfect' body out of thin air because it doesn't exist.

I'll spare you a serving of cliché and won't say that you're perfect the way you are, because you aren't. Neither am I, neither is your ex, neither is your GBF. 'Perfect' is a mirage; it's something we run towards but never reach because it isn't there (okay, that was a cliché.)

We need to stop setting our standards so high. We need to stop telling ourselves: 'You could be pretty if...'; 'You would look beautiful when...'; 'Your body would look amazing after...'

We need to stop being so judgmental about the looks of our LGBTI brothers and sisters. Most of all, we need to realize that eating disorders can ruin the lives of men and woman and we need to support those who struggle with one.

## The Curse of the First Date Fuck.

For gay men, dating can be a tricky thing. Usually the guy you want to stick around never does, and the ones you don't want to see again spend the next four months trying to shoehorn their way back into your life. First dates are even trickier still: drawn-out silences, waiting for his first genuine smile... and of course we're often faced with the question: Should we f*ck, or should we wait?

The curse of the first date f*ck - it's a conundrum: Do we give it up easy and thus risk putting him off, or do we restrain from getting down and dirty but maybe miss out on hot sex? Top, bottom, vers...it's possible we aren't compatible anyway! Do we trust our instinct and assume there's real chemistry between us? Does he like our personality as much as we like his? Let's hold off for something more meaningful, we don't want him thinking we're a ho. But what if there's no connection? He's hot, so let's fuck anyway? I mean, we're both here now. If this strikes you as a trivial subject to write about, you're wrong. Really. Bollocks to the rest of you, because many of us have fallen victim to the curse of the first date f*ck.

Let me tell you a story.

We'd been chatting for a while and the conversation was easy, it just flowed effortlessly. There's nothing worse than stale or forced banter, it's like having your teeth yanked at by Katie Hopkins as she slowly reads her tweets aloud. A good connection in these days of dick pics and poor spelling is rare, so I pounced on it. I really liked this guy. Well, perhaps that's an exaggeration, our first date was the only time we'd spent together because, like all other feisty millennials, we met on Twitter.

A week or so later we met up for drinks. As the evening ticked by, I found myself lured into a false sense of security. We switched bars, we drank more. We looked each other dead in the eye. His gaze didn't even waver when I felt his hand brush up my inner thigh. We had one more drink then took a taxi back to his. We slept together.

After that night whenever I tried to make plans with him he'd always be 'busy.' Even if he'd posted a Snapchat saying he was bored, or Tweeted that he wanted plans, he was always busy when it came to me. This excuse made approximately 0.1% sense. One thing was definite: I slept with him and it ruined the chance of something real happening. I felt like an idiot.

There's a lot of antiquated ideas about dating floating around, and first-date sex is often a topic of controversy, with many people still attaching a shameful stigma to it. Just for clarity, I don't have an issue with it. If someone wants to have sex on the first date go for it. The 'curse' I am referring to is the one that is cast after you've slept together. The one that sees the spark fizzle into nothingness; when you wake up the next day and the chemistry just vanishes. We've all been there: a few too many drinks, you wind up going back to the guy's place; you stumble into his room and he follows behind, gently closing the door so he doesn't wake his flatmate, both of you giggling annoyingly. You peel off your t-shirt, an attempt to match him sliding off his jeans. Next thing he's on top of you, panting like a parched dog, grinding, drooling into your ear. He's saying all the things he wants to do to you, and you're thinking '*I wish I'd kept my trainers on so I could make my getaway.*'

Despite him having a good job, a great body and seemingly being a nice guy, the sex is awkward. It's sweaty, kind of uncomfortable. It feels like he's just stabbing in the dark and hoping it'll go in. You don't know him, he doesn't know you. Eventually he finishes, and so does your first date. You lie there, trying to resurrect the chemistry, but it's gone. You arrange to hangout again next week. You order an Uber and leave.

You chalk the mediocre sex up to being quite drunk;

surely any awkwardness between the sheets will be excused? Besides you got on so well! A couple of days pass, you hear nothing. You text him, both drunk and sober, nada. Zilch. You start suffering some kind of OCD compulsion to repetitively check your phone. Still nothing. This goes on and on until somewhere around day nine when you are contemplating the sexual equivalent of an annulment, he replies saying 'SORRY', and that he's been 'BUSY'. It feels like your balls had been dragged along a gravel path and slammed in a car door.

The truth is, one awkward experience between the sheets can stop one, if not both, of the parties from wanting to meet up again. Someone can seem perfect on Twitter, but in reality things may take longer to blossom. Forming a connection with someone whilst hidden behind a phone screen is simpler for some of us. Being confident with your naked body is easier over Snapchat as you control what the other person sees. When we're presented with the face-to-face reality though it is very different. A lot of us fear that the guy won't find us interesting enough for a second date, so we put out in the hope that'll be enough to give us a chance to see him again. But if he doesn't find you interesting then surely he's not worth sleeping with anyway?

Every time it's happened to me, I'd spend the next night thrashing round in bed, like a confused and angry animal, slapping my headboard in frustration. Passing out after six hours of slowly analysing how I poisoned this relationship, only to lurch awake 45 minutes later. I can't quite work out what's worse: the fact he stopped talking to me after we slept together or the fact I slept with him after only meeting for a few hours?

Sex on the first date isn't guaranteed to destroy a bidding romance. I know couples that met, fucked, and are still together, so there's definitely not a science behind it. The curse of the first date fuck is more of a cautionary tale, one we tell friends and twinks so they don't misbehave. To me I see it more as guidelines, and these days I try to stick to those guidelines. If that person is really into you, he will want to see you again. If it's meant to be, then you'll have plenty time for sex.

Sadly, until hindsight kicks in, sometimes you're damned to whip yourself over a mistake that doesn't actually exist. Despite my views, and possibly isolated story, the curse of the first date f*ck will continue to be perpetuated. As long as there are people who are anxious in the bedroom, and those who blame themselves for each mishap, and those who really only wanted sex all along, it'll continue. We will employ a reason for it not working out, and that reason is 'it's our fault.' When really we just need to be careful.

# Ghosted.

It's so easy to blame yourself when a date goes full-blown Brexit. Sometimes this happens, dates go tits up and then you wind up wondering why. I know I do: 'I AM TOO AWKWARD AND HAVE TERRIBLE BANTER', 'SLEEPING WITH ME MUST HAVE FELT LIKE FIGHTING A DECK CHAIR', 'I AM THE SEXUAL EQUIVALENT OF A WHITE PERSON RAPPING.' The sorrow and humiliation is overpowering, but sometimes it's just a case of it didn't work out. Sometimes lust gets the better of you and sometimes the other person doesn't feel a spark. I mean, sure, SOMETIMES the guy is a charlatan that wanted nothing but sex, then after the deed is done he disappears like the mangy sewer rat he is. In that case the sex itself isn't to blame, neither are you: He is.

Without a doubt some guys handle the situation poorly. They ghost you, make lame excuses, even go out on dates with other people - thanks a lot, you absolute joy thieves. When things go wrong it's easy to see situations through the rose-tinted glasses of 'what if'. Someone can seem like 'THE ONE THAT GOT AWAY' because it ended quicker than it started, but is that because you rushed things sexually? Or because there simply wasn't that connection? Feelings, love, sex, all can be genuinely awful. Like the norovirus on a coach trip. That's why you need to protect yourself.

# PrEP Talk.

As I climbed the cold stairs to the sexual-health clinic I felt as though I was going insane. With each step I promised myself that if I can just get another all clear, be handed a clean bill of sexual health, I'd change my ways. I'd become a good gay. I'd stop the string of random hook-ups, I'd invest time in love and hold out for that 'big relationship.' No longer would I have to anxiously white-knuckle my way through another blood test.

This wasn't the way life was meant to be; when I was younger I bought into an illusion that gay life in was a whirlwind of casual, yet mind-blowing, sex. Carefree, void of any negative consequences. Then I racked up some field time; I gained some traction as to how sex really works. When I become aware of all the potential dangers that comes with it, that illusion quickly deflated. I attribute a large part of this ignorance to the lack of LGBTQ + inclusive sex education, but that's another matter.

So here I am, again. In this frosty waiting room. Sitting with my legs crossed, terror trickling down my throat and sitting uncomfortably in the pit of my stomach. Trying to ignore the judgemental sneer I feel deep in my bones, praying that I'll get away with it this time. Then it happens, someone I know walks in. Half the thoughts in my head have assembled are now screaming at me to jump out of the window; the other half are urging me to bury my face in my phone screen, which I do. And for the next few minutes I sit emanating one gruff, depressing sigh after another, sweating, panicking.

Then she comes out. The nurse glances around the waiting

room, then calls my name, 'Christopher?' With that she'd unmasked the anonymity I'd hoped to gain by shielding my face with my phone.

Idly I'm chatting away to the nurse as she does my bloods. I have shy veins, and a horrible faint-inducing-phobia of needles, so she distracts with me a series of questions. *'How many sexual partners have you had over the last few months?'* 'Do you feel that you put myself in potentially hazards situations?' And 'Having you been watching celebrity Big Brother?'Then it comes, the question I've been hoping to avoid the same way you do a racist relative. *'Have anyone spoken to you about PrEP?'* She mutters casually, as though asking what I'm having for dinner. I am seized by a sharp, cold dread. This didn't feel like a casual conversation anymore, more like a hostage situation. The confusion I felt was overwhelming; Why is he asking me this? Do I have that many sexual partners? Is my personal life that much of a mess that I need to take extra percussions?

After sharing these concerns and questions with the nurse, who was now looking at me as though I was teetering on the verge of an imminent breakdown, it turns out the answer was no. Why? Because there is no such thing as too man partners. There isn't a scale where after you've bedded a certain amount of people you earn your 'slut' badge. The nurse and I sit and chat, as if we though we're simply too adults having a normal conversation – because that's what we are doing, having a normal conversation about sexual-health. Suddenly my full dissociated meltdown subsides, and I realise there's no judgment here, there's no scrutiny.

My issue was never with PrEP, that's not what's caused this sudden panic. My response to the drug being accessible on the NHS was nothing but enthusiastic. What's caused the panic is the stigma attached to being on PrEP, and the negative comments other gay men are all so willing to give about it. The conversation continues, and I realise on an intellectual level that I've been lied to. By papers, by adults, by former teachers. By Facebook, by the unwanted opinions of other gay men, of other people. This perpetual stigma attached to sexual heath is now wrapping itself around PrEP and those who choose to use it.

There's so much misinformation about sexual health, about this drug, floating around out there. *'You don't need PrEP just wear a condom!'* Condom's only stop 70% of HIV infections. It's this sort of mentality that adds to the stigma. It causes people to have visions of wanton orgies worthy of vintage gay porn whenever someone tells them they're on PrEP. That's not fair.

The conversation concludes with me telling the nurse that on the few occasions I have taken a random home I normally just actively encourage him to spoon me, before falling sleeping, and probably snoring like a warthog. And that I don't have a bucket-load of men lining up to worship my every pube. The reality is I've only slept with two people in the last six months. It was nothing but blind panic and fear of judgment that caused my meltdown earlier. From this we deduce that PrEP isn't needed in my case. As I go to leave the clinic, the guy I know gets called, we exchange a smile, and with that we kick stigma out the window I considered jumping from earlier. We should all be confident that we're just humans who are looking after their health, and sexual health is just as important as anything else. And that should never merit any form of negativity or stigma.

## Scared of Happy.

I have uttered the words 'I love you' to precisely three guys, not including male relatives, my dad or assorted platonic neurotics I get drunk with. The first I have tortured enough on the public forum, so I will not rehash our affairs here. Suffice to say, I told him of my feelings first, and he did not reciprocate, he just sent a shady ass message via Facebook. It took long spells of crying and begging before he relented and apologised for hurting me, but by that time the words had lost their charm. OVER IT!

The second didn't pan out much better. His questionable interest and shaky sexuality put a strain on the relationship from the get go. I felt like I was dating a spy the entire time we were together. I'd try to kiss him on the walk home and he'd say 'SOMEONE COULD SEE US' before bounding four steps ahead of me. When I tried to cuddle into him, it felt like I was spooning a disinterested rock. The night he finally said it back we had snuck off to a bedroom as the party started to wind down. As I was straddling him on a desk chair he blurted out 'I LOVE YOU'. I declined to answer him. Next day we lay in bed and ate too much. I cried, he pretended not to see it. I cried again, ostensibly because

I missed him even though he was inches away and also because I know he didn't mean those three slurred words the night before.

Also, I have IBS, so that and pizza are not two folks you want together at a party.

The third sort of operated on a different level. The story has everything: drama, drunkenness, jealousy, ended friendships and cat sitting. At first it felt like more of a long crush that made the days go quicker and fulfilled my need for a raging summer lust. Then Autumn crept in and I realised that I was way too attached. Unfortunately for me he also realised this and soon he was telling me he couldn't cum from blow jobs, that he'd slept with other guys, and then generally started avoiding me. Once he even pretended his kitchen caught fire to get out of plans.

The thought of possibly reaching that stage again, and taking that total up to four, fills me with both glee and pant-shitting fear. I somehow always ruin things. Then they somehow ruin things more by cutting contact. As gay men I feel there's this pathological need to sabotage any chance of happiness from a healthy relationship that we may have. I think I know why. When we were younger, growing up and going through puberty, we were never told as boys that it is okay to one day say 'I love you' to another guy. I had PDA from straight-couples thrown in my face and spent most my days watching hetero-relationships blossom. Every time I turned a corner in high school, and for years after that too, it was straight up breeder love. It was like watching a Meg Ryan and Hugh Grant romance movie on loop eternally.

I'd sit completely alone in the playground and watch the

practice of normality unfold around me. How many of us spent years watching straight couples explore their sexuality and the whole time felt like a homeless man? Avoidable, unseen and begging for change.

When you're forced to conform to the 'social norm' like that your sense of pride in your sexuality shrinks. So now, when a romance threatens to bloom, somehow subconsciously, and often quite spectacularly, we royally fuck it up. Because on some level so many gay guys still don't believe that we deserve love or can have it.

Extensive scientific research has proven that if you're unattainable and removed from sleazy meat-market that is the single-gay dating experience, then suddenly everyone becomes interested in you – why? Because people always want what they can't have.

So many gay guys I know go after boys in relationships because of the reasons I mentioned earlier: They don't feel it's okay for them to be happy with a guy, so they chase after something that is fated to be doomed and finite. Chasing after happiness because we know we won't catch it is like yelling 'fight me' to someone when they're too far away to hear.

Life is long, and there are good guys out there, we just happen to be looking in all the wrong places. Then somehow we meet a good guy; a gold-star gay with a big dick and bigger heart; whose hopes and dreams mirror our own. How many of us ruin things because we think we aren't good enough for that guy? A guy that has already proclaimed his affection for you. It could be going great then self-doubt reminds us that there is someone better than ourselves. There's someone hotter than me or more successful or, fuck knows, who can breathe fire. Or we find faults in him, we conjure up reasons that it wouldn't work. Why are we scared of happy? Wouldn't it be nice that the next time we say 'I love you' to someone, they want to say it back?

# *Section III*

# Heartache & Healing

## Toothbrush.

I vow to never have sex with anyone again until it's with someone that I am in love with. I wait a few weeks before shattering this vow, and then also my dignity. But it happened and out of the blue I fell in love. It's not like in the movies though. There were no flowers, or romantic strolls along beaches that are so beautiful they almost seem fictitious. There's no stimulating dialog or public displays of affection. Reality showed up with a shiny, razor-sharp pin and popped that bubble. Yet, I am in love.

When he texts me he's normally abrupt. Each message is laced with a general sense of indifference toward both the conversation and me – unless, of course, he wants something. When he turns up at my flat in the middle of night, it's not done as a heart-felt gesture or a need to show me he cares; it's done because he's white girl wasted. He staggers up my hallway, fumbling from side-to-side. He resembles a human tennis ball being batted back and forth by the walls. I go through to the kitchen to get him some water and by the time I come back through he's slumped in a drunken heap on top of my bed, fully clothed, tangled up in my two-meter long phone charger. His friends have left him, he's really drunk, he has obliterated his phone screen and the battery has also died.

Not four hours ago, I found out he was posting snippets of our private conversations on his Twitter and making fun of me. I confronted him about it, but the issue remained unresolved. Yet here he is, stinking of alcohol, caked in make-up, waking me up in the middle of night; dressed in tight clothes and armed with fleeting affection.

I look down at him upon my bed and he's still sporting that infectiously cheeky smile. He mumbles *'I know you hate me right now'*, but then follows with *'I have nowhere to go.'*

The truth of the matter is I don't hate him, I love him. I'm angry as hell at him because he's treated my heart like monkey meat for the last few months, but I don't hate him. The opposite of love isn't hate, it's indifference, and there's no way I could ever be blasé about his existence.

He lies there silent, squinting at his phone, looking at it the way an addict would crack if it was being flushed down the toilet. Rather than speak to me or explain, or even offer up an apology, he just glares into the screen which illuminates his drunk, fake-tanned face. I ask what his plans are, if he's staying over or do I need to get him a taxi home. He opts for the latter. I'm a mixture of relived and hurt.

He starts falling asleep, so I wake him up when his ride arrives, but not before I stop and look at him. Not in a creepy way, well not overtly creepy anyway, but rather in a way to says 'I adore you' because a pissed off as I am he's still my future.

His taxi arrives and he is once again zig-zagging down my hallway, using my body as a crutch, out my door and, after the next couple of days, out my life.

I stay awake and wait for him to let me know he's home safe. An hour passes and I hear nothing. I call, but his phone is switched off. I lay on my bed in a way that's only acceptable if you've been in a bad accident or you've been crippled by seasonal depression. My mood is a concoction of anxiety, anger and arousal but then my attention is grabbed away. I notice my pillow reeks of alcohol and an unfamiliar aftershave.

It's not my aftershave and it's not his aftershave - I know this because I bought him his aftershave – which means he's been with another guy tonight. I sob, partially from picturing him being with someone else and also because I hate the way I am expressing myself. Maybe I'm too attached to know what thoughts are useless to me. I have all the knowledge but none of the language to get myself out of this situation. I am not angry that I love him, I am just angry that I don't have better words.

The next afternoon my heart still hurts. When I eat my lunch, when I'm at work, there's this constant dull ache in my chest. We've spent the day arguing about what I feel his behaviour is, and what I feel it should be. I try and explain his actions have consequences, but he's a seasoned actor when it comes to playing the victim, so my words rang unheard.

I sit and think back to all the times he's made me feel worthless and all the times he's made me feel good – both through sex and words. The bad is outweighing the good here. I sit and I think about him at this party the other night, his wily eyes trained on another guy; his smooth hands touching someone else's body. His lips pressed again someone else's mouth or, worse, placed elsewhere. I feel as though there's a bowling ball in my stomach.

I find out while at work that night that he'd lied - he did

hook up with another guy. He's only telling me because he has since learned that this guy has an STD, but it's okay because they are going to get tested together – how romantic.

My anxiety is incorrigible; out of control. The fact he has had unsafe sex with someone he barely knows, then lied about it, loops in my head. Who else has he been with and not told me? I feel I've been made a fool off. I try to cry even though I don't want to, but I know it'll be cathartic.

Right now, I don't feel I am being clear about my pain. I am told by my friends that this guy is trouble, he's not a good person, that none of this is my fault. Their opinion doesn't mirror his though; he makes me feel as though there are at least ten different ways that this is all my fault. I misread things, I got attached, I'm too needy – just some of the reasons he gives for his behaviour toward me. A couple of weeks later I found out that he had been sending nudes to other people, that he had been messing around with other guys and that on my birthday he made out with my friend while I was away getting us drinks.

I'm back home now, sitting on my sofa. I allow my mind to wonder back and revisit the last few months, replaying every scene he's been in and scrutinizing it as though I am searching for some vital piece of information I may have overlooked. Every conversation we've had I go back to; I analyse every time we were intimate, searching desperately for an explanation that'll justify why he doesn't feel the same way back – I need a reason, I can't rest without one.

I offered him honest and impartial advice on every subject

under the sun. I leant him money, I bought him nice gifts. I made sure he knew how gorgeous he was every day. I asked for nothing in return. I thought I did it right this time…but I never got to utter the words 'I love you' to him, not directly. I said it over the phone, over Twitter, over iMessage; but never to his face. I think such a blatant display of affection may have sent him over the edge.

He let me buy him things, he let me be close to him. Whenever I held him or spooned him I felt as though I was clinging onto my future; trying desperately to stop it wriggling away. I knew it would never work though, deep down I knew; and there was no chance of reconciliation after all of this, so I took all the clichéd measures required to get over it.

I deleted all 54 photos of him off my phone (both clothed and unclothed.) The picture frame he gave me for my birthday which had a photo of him in it with "Your 1 and only" etched across it in black marker pen has since wound up in the bin. I decided to not remove him from my life by blocking him on every platform possible, but rather just to distance myself.

I done all this and I feel good. I feel sad, stingy almost, but I know I am doing the right thing. I start feeling like me again, so I organised to meet a friend for a coffee; I wanted to celebrate my new-found liberty from heartache.

I went to get ready, got dressed and downed my fifth cup of tea that day. I ventured into the bathroom and checked the mirror, a final once-over. My attention is pulled down by a flash of colour lingering deviously in the corner of my eye. There it was, his toothbrush, regally standing next to mine. A little orange reminder that he had been here, in my life, in my flat, in my heart.

I threw the toothbrush out. I felt like it was kind of a juvenile thing to do; that it was sad and petty. But I also felt that it was a psychical reaction to a very real emotional pain. I felt it was kind of symbolic. I felt it needed to be done.

# 18

Loneliness is a funny thing. Solitude, aloneness, singleness. If you live loneliness for so long after a while it becomes an actual ache in your bones. It's a mode of existence that comes very naturally to me. The sort of loneliness that allows you to ponder and dream about what things would be like if you were still with someone you were once in love with. The one where you imagine the simple things you'd do together. How you'd be shopping together, in the car together, holding hands together. Just those things that are so simplistic in their beauty but are always taken for granted in a relationship.

It's not until now, a year since I first started speaking to the last person I was in love with, that I'm able to look back at what we had and how we handled it in a way that's equal parts of satisfying and sad.

There was a noticeable age gap, and when we first got together my bedroom felt like it had no windows in it. At the start I thought, this is kind of cool, it's like we're on a boat; it's exciting, new, almost an adventure -  but at the time I was unaware that I was wading into waters too deep to swim in.

It felt like this because he was younger, and this fact caused me to handle him delicately like I would a kitten. We kissed each other before we tumbled into my bed for what I thought would be a one-off thing. What I didn't know at the time was that there we'd stay intermittently for the next few months; leaving every other day only for sustenance, work or when he had to go to college. Once I asked him to take a selfie with me after sex, as proof of how young and rosy we were, but the picture came out as shadowy as the relationship would soon turn out to be.

Every time I left him I felt uneasy and afraid; the outside light hurting my eyes like I'd been stuck in that windowless room for years. Whenever he left an unknown fear crept in and it caused me to panic that something bad would happen to him in my absence. That someone else would discover how perfect he was.

After he'd stayed a few times and became comfortable in my bed, he started asking me to take the side against the wall – the opposite side of where I usually slept. Quite often I'd shoot awake in the middle of the night sweaty and disoriented, my face pressed against plaster. *'This isn't working'* I thought, as I tossed and turned, cuddling up with my discomfort and insomnia as he overheated when I hugged into him.

The first night we went out together it became clear to me how ill-matched we were. The moment we were in a place that wasn't the comfort of my unmade bed we began to crumble. Aspects of our personality, which had remained buried in the sheets until this point, started to surface. He got mean, I got sad. He flew around the room, flirting shamelessly with others, I drank too much and got jealous. After that evening I was left entertaining the idea that we were only connected by our bodies, wedged together by my king-sized bed.

Over the next eight weeks we stopped and started, wept and slept. We'd fight and go to bed angry then I'd awake with a gasp and listen to his breathing, terrified he'd left during the night. I felt trapped in a place between space and time, one from which I couldn't leave. I was stuck in a windowless room and I couldn't breathe - I just had to exist there.

One frosty December morning he left to go to college, exiting my flat via my wardrobe and wallet, withdrawing enough money to make sure he'd be able to get food for that day and his train fare home; borrowing clothes that were 'too expensive' for him to afford. When he was gone I looked in the mirror, my hair tangled, my eyes housed blacked circles and my mouth felt like the Sahara. I wasn't sleeping, I wasn't eating. A constellation of broken capillaries decorated my eyes. I was hiding this 'relationship' from every single one of my friends and like all secrets, it was starting to take its toll.

*'What's happening to you?'* I said aloud.

It's hard to give up on someone you really care about, even if you know it's not going to last forever.

*'I think I'm in love with him.'* If my reflection could scoff without me noticing, he probably would have. We both knew it wasn't going to work.

I tried to close my eyes and surgically remove the thought of the inevitable future I'd soon face. I felt snippets of my sanity slithering away. It's hard to believe that something as simple as the concept of love could cede such carnage in its wake. It's even harder to believe that a difference in age could weave such a tangled web.

I looked across at our seemingly bleak horizon. I pictured my future and imagined being strapped to a gurney in a mental hospital, my heart as antiqued and rusted as the machine they'd use on me for electroshock therapy. Driven insane by a promise I knew he could never keep and by the secrets I was harbouring,

Three weeks later our relationship concluded. I sat looking at my phone trying to convince myself that I didn't know the pass-code to unlock it; when in reality I didn't even have one set at the time. With shaky finality I crafted my goodbyes as elegantly as iMessage would allow. Shortly after his response came through, and I shivered as his cold reply ran through my entire body. He pretended he didn't care and so that final nail-in-the-coffin feeling arrived.

For a solid hour after I felt trapped within the white confines of my room; as though I had just let my freedom go, as if my second chance was now on death row. I sat on the edge of my bed, my head between my knees, the international sign for panic attack, and wept between gasping breaths.

Seven months on since our relationship ended and I am clinging to some of our memories like I would my backpack in a bad part of town; worried-but-happy at the knowledge that, for now, its contents are safe.

I never believed that I'd have choices in love, or that I

deserved them. That guys like me - awkward, begging guys - can be the ones to walk away from a relationship. I left my last heartbreak armed with the knowledge that there will always be choices, and windows, for guys like me and that I'll never have to sleep against the wall again.

## Shout Out to my Ex.

He's talking about love, but he's only known me a few months. He's attractive, caring. He's well employed and is a damn good cook. I should have known it was going too well – a general rule of thumb, if something seems too good to be true then it probably is.

He messages me every morning to say he misses me, and then again asking if he can come over that night. I like my own space, but the more time I spend in his orbit the more frequently I'm saying 'yes' to this request. On paper, he's the perfect boyfriend; the type of guy you wouldn't hesitate to take home to the parents. His charm, his wit, his ability to make conversation with anyone…He exudes confidence.

But first impressions are finite; nothing more than a quick glimpse into a showroom – a fleeting introduction tailored to fit the occasion. The more you explore someone, the more they change. This is true for you.

You're currently away in London; a holiday you've had planned since before we met. On this trip, you're accompanied by an American guy; a person you've never met yet claim to talk to everyday. This guy flew over from the good old US of A just to meet my boyfriend. He's also a solid ten; a fucking walking Adonis straight off Instagram, complete with filter. I try to articulate my concerns and issues with this, but it's hard to reach a resolution when the person doesn't reply – and you never reply.

I sit and contemplate this behaviour because when we are together, you're so there, and so present; and then suddenly you disappear for day or so, don't answer any of my texts or calls, and I feel as though I invented you. You say you've been busy partying and hanging out, that's why you haven't replied. I won't apologise for expecting a little effort.

I explained that you can't bench your boyfriend whilst you jet off on some booze-filled holiday with a random guy that you've never met. You can't put me on hold for nine days. You can't be sharing a bed with another guy this whole trip.

When I woke up that morning and scrolled through your Snapchat story the smell was unmistakable: Betrayal. There you were, arm slung affectionately around the guy you told me not to worry about, with a cluster of hearts decorating the picture. This was the first of many pictures, and as more were uploaded during the days that followed I found myself wondering, 'Is he going to apologise for this?'

With the legal prowess and endless cool of a hot-shot TV-show lawyer, I rhyme off facts and fears to a court of my peers in the hope they'll help me reach a verdict. I'm just waiting to find out what's happening, waiting to get more facts about who you are. Waiting to be free from the recurrence of obsessive thoughts and the milky, sickening feeling I get when I think of you sleeping beside someone else. The Jury is out: I know you've cheated.

I have no native skill except to make mistakes – this I know. However, I can accept full responsibility for when I fuck up. You, on the other hand, cannot. If there's been one constant during the time that I've known you, it's your complete absence of responsibility. As if the above wasn't bad enough, you then started making me think that I was in the wrong; that it was all my fault. Sure, it's totally my mental health issues that I've been really open about and not your secretive trip to London to meet a guy who's literally flown from America to see you. It's completely my fault we fell apart, and not you leaving the country to go to a city that's an eight hour train journey away to spend nine days with a guy from the internet that you 'speak to every day.' It's couldn't be, let's say, your borderline split personality and astounding lack of scruples?

Here's an idea, why don't you place one crumb of basic human compassion on that fat-free muffin of sociopathic detachment you've been chomping on and see how it tastes? Make a note of this now. On your brain. With a sharp stick. And try not to poke the bit that switches your cock on while you're up there:

You are a shallow, cheating, priapic skunk. A guy that would fuck a McChicken Sandwich if no one was looking. Sex is all you care about. It's the only thing. There's literally nothing else going on in your mind. Remove those thoughts and your skull would likely cave in. And if you say otherwise to a guy, then you're lying in the hope that your weedy excuses with ensnare that

poor boy into a false sense of security, and you can have your way
with him – in a bathroom cubicle if needs me.

You're quasi-sentient jizz box; a walking cum dispenser.
You care about someone's feelings until you get what you want
and then throw them away like a shit-stained baby wipe and, like
most cheaters, lack the maturity to take ownership.

Infuriatingly enough this is all stuff I want to say to you,
but I can't because you've swiftly removed me from all social
media and added my number to your block list – congratulations
on avoiding responsibility with such showy, sugary gusto, you
morally bankrupt dick-swinger.


## Two Princes.

There are two ways into someone's heart; one leads us there
through the validation of time, the other through darkened tunnels
of addiction and infatuation. One is earned, the other is a trick, but
by random universal symmetry both routes lead to the same place:
the feeling that something is missing.

I think about the feasibility of this, whilst cradling my tea
with the same fragility I would a new-born. I think about my heart
and the pockmarks and stains that now decorate it; the scars its
earned from years of enthusiastically handing it around. The trials
of time have weakened its walls, seeing it passed back to me in a
worse condition. There have been many names doodled on it
throughout my life, with the latest always standing out in bold –
*yours*. I didn't want to love you then, and I still don't want to

love you now. I've moved on; accepted that we were finite and made peace with our relationship's sad trajectory. Then we spoke again, recently, before drunkenly tumbling into mistakes we promised wouldn't happen again. I remember how it felt the first time and compare it to how it feels now.

I sit and dismantle that memory, brick-by-boring-brick. I imagine rebuilding it, recreating us, but this time miles away. Away from the unwanted opinions of our families, away from sharp remarks from our peers. I imagine, once its rebuilt, all the ways that I could have kept you. I could move in when you weren't looking, barricade myself inside your life and just wait for you to come home.

I'd be sitting cross-legged on the floor, and wordlessly I'd welcome you, my grasp of your language so delicate that my voice threatened to break. You'd fold yourself into my lap and there we'd stay, fingers intertwined, our worlds merging. I'd whisper, *'I love you'* just one more time. My words would hang in the air, consequence waiting to descend upon me. I know this emotion well: the uneasy silence of unrequited love. But in this new life I'd built you'd say it back and I could finally breathe again.

But reality comes like the onset of a flu, and a sickly sensation snatches away that possibility. It doesn't work like that – it didn't work like that – I know it couldn't work like that. So why am I still holding onto something that leads me by the hand to tears?

Every time I look at you or even hear someone say your name, I feel an ominous rot in the pit of my stomach. I'm just waiting to hear that you've moved on, or for news of your sex life to be dropped into casual conversation. My friends want to know why I still care; why I still come to your aid like a prince in a fairy-tale - but I always know why.

I recognise in you something I was denied when I was younger; a love that wasn't mine, an opportunity I wasn't able to take. When we first met the age-gap showcased how far the LGBT community has come in terms of self-expression, equality and acceptance. I'd never have been as comfortable in my skin then as you are now. You are everything now that I wish I was then. That's why I wanted to keep you; to finally get the chance to rewrite that story. I wanted to live through you the life I couldn't when I was younger. I wanted to be loved now because I wasn't then. It wasn't so long ago that it's seen as history, but the differences in time and our ages made it feel like we were centuries apart.

Today, I miss you in every way. I miss you swinging between belittlement and sugary praise; the way you kept me weak and dependent, like all young drugs do. The sleepless nights after never ending fights. I miss holding you. I miss kissing you. I miss how baggy my sweater was hanging over your skinny frame. Every time I see your face, I imagine your heart, paler than its usual pale, missing beats, missing us, missing me.

We were almost content, finally. Two princes, kingdoms apart, trying their hardest to ignore disaster. The people around us said we were doomed from the start, so we kept every touch a secret. And through hidden tunnels you found your way into my heart; but you were too young and I was too bold; what I wanted you simply didn't know how to give. Now I navigate cautiously around our wreckage, looking for pieces of a crown that didn't fit.

## Heal Over.

It's easy to forget someone's magic when they're no longer in your life. Their faults, mistakes and indiscretions become a narrative louder than "Remember how happy he once made you." Those times they made you feel amazing are now foggy and time-worn; the passionate sex is a dimly lit, bland memory. Yes, it's easier to villainise and critique, to condemn and resent; to forget the glimmering fantasy-land you once shared. It's simpler to do this than it is to heal and forgive; because when you still carry a torch for someone, holding onto the terrible ways they treated you is sometimes the only thing keeping what you had alive.

One of the worst feelings in the world is feeling unwanted by the person you once wanted the most. They say breaking up with someone you love is one of the most difficult and potent aches you'll ever experience, but I'd like to challenge that. For me, it isn't the breakup itself; nor is it the wise and somewhat jaded "posting inspirational things about love on social media" stage. No, I find that the hardest part comes after the separation; it occurs a few months, maybe even a year, down the line. It's the part when you see them with someone else, someone new. That's a sobering moment, one in which you realise they've moved on while you've been standing still.

Accepting that someone else now makes your ex happy isn't an easy, it makes you feel as though there's a pit in your stomach. This happened to me recently, in a bar, unexpectedly, on a cold and crisp night, while out for a few drinks.

I knew he had moved on; I'd heard about it from friends, from his other-ex and from enemies. I'd be surfing Instagram, peering in at the lives of people I don't know, and I'd stumble upon several cute pictures of him with his new partner. I'd attempted to ignore it, but like a rash it was all over my social media, taunting me. No matter how hard I tried to cover it up or make it go away, it just seemed to spread.

The reality was quite different though. The encounter was brief, and for that I am eternally thankful; but despite being fleeting it was long enough to fill my head full of hodgepodge thoughts and leave it spinning for a few days. Amid the mayhem of this moment one thing caught my eye: He appeared settled with this new guy. I don't know the dynamics of his new relationship; their story was unreadable to me. But what I could loosely translate was something that seemed like happiness – their happiness, not 'ours.'

After seeing them I felt a need so immediate it was like demanding that a bus driver pullover, so I could go to the bathroom despite being in the middle of a manic highway. I wanted to know: 'What did I do wrong?' Why was it 'them', and not 'us'? And how do I accept that the short string of guys I once loved found happiness and warmth in the embrace of someone else? I never asked him the questions, I just assumed this is the game of love and I am no good at it.

After a breakup, my take is always 'I loved him too much' and I feel in this case there's a sharp truth to that. I perhaps did love him too much, in way that he wasn't ready for, in a style that didn't suit him. I always knew that after things ended we'd slip away from each other in a series of impossibly tiny steps. What I didn't prepare myself for was how much he'd change, and how quickly it would happen.

Yet I remain the same. And I am no less heartbroken.

I am not saying I want him or any of my exes back. But to me love is a really cool, powerful, lasting thing and it doesn't have to be defined the way Western Culture define it as 'beginnings' and 'ends.' But something snapped when I saw them together. Maybe it was the feeling of barely recognising someone I once thought I wanted to spend my life with. Perhaps it was being told these new relationships were 100 percent happiness, but after studying them for clues realising that these new guys aren't treating them any worse or better than I did.

The gap between what I believe I contribute to a relationship and what actually unfolds is widening. In order to close it, I need to roll up my sleeves and get to work. Change my behaviour and dysmorphic perceptions. I will work my ass off to re-parent myself, to work out where I went in wrong. To sieve out what faults were solely mine, but also to acknowledge that I am not entirely to blame and sometimes, it really is them and not me.

I always say that holding onto anything toxic is what stops

you from growing as a person. If you see your ex with someone else, it's okay to feel hurt or even heartbroken. It's alright if you need to listen to sad songs and cry it out but accept it's over and be happy for them.

In the mean time I will continue to find happiness for my exes, no matter how deep down I have to dig. When images or posts pop up on my feed, I'll silently support the new relationships they venture into. I am many things, but I am not bitter. I won't wait for them any longer, but I also won't harbour any feeling of negativity.

For more follow Topher on Twitter @TopherJGen or check out his site www.tophergen.com

Printed in Great Britain
by Amazon

65390960R00043